ROMAN ADVENTURE
Activity Book

Illustrated by Jen Alliston

Button BOOKS

Thousands of years ago, the city of Rome became very powerful. Roman armies took control of many countries, creating a mighty empire. This book is packed with activities to help you find out more about Ancient Rome, from daily life to deadly combat in the arena. Get ready for heaps of fun involving all sorts of characters, from evil emperors to legendary legionaries and great gods.

Double trouble (the founding of Rome)

Use words from the sticker page to complete the story.

According to legend, Rome was founded in [   ] by twin [   ]

Romulus and Remus. The boys were the sons of [   ], the god of war. When

they were [   ], their wicked uncle threw them into the [   ].

They were saved by a [   ]. When the boys

grew up, Mars told them to build a [   ] on the

riverbank. But they had a [   ] and Romulus killed

Remus, so the city was named after Romulus!

Find the Roman villa

Help the archaeologist find the Roman villa.

What the Romans did for us

The Romans were great at making things. What they didn't invent, they copied and improved and then introduced throughout the empire. Some things we still use today were developed by the Romans. Choose words from the list and write the correct one by each picture. Can you think of anything else the Romans are famous for?

Daily news

Alphabet

Aqueduct

Months of the year

Public toilets

_ _ _ _ _ _ _ _

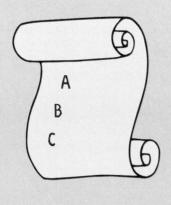

_ _ _ _ _ _ _

_ _ _ _ _ _ _

_ _ _ _ _

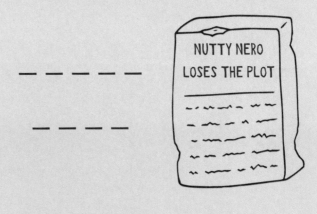

NUTTY NERO LOSES THE PLOT

_ _ _ _ _ _ _

JULY

_ _ _ _ _ _ _ _ _ _ _

_ _ _ _ _ _ _ _ _ _

_ _ _ _ _

Who's who in Ancient Rome

Can you match these people to their descriptions below?

---------- ----------

Patricians

Rich people were called patricians. They were landowners and senators (government officials). Men wore long white robes called togas. Women wore ankle-length tunics and shawls over the top, fastened with brooches.

Slave

Slaves were people who had been captured by soldiers, pirates, or slave traders. There were millions of slaves in the empire. They worked very hard and were owned by a master or mistress. This slave is wearing a tunic with a blue belt and carrying a jug.

- - - - -   - - - - - - -   - - - - -

Emperor

After 27 BC, the Roman government was led by an emperor. Some emperors were very good, while others were very bad. This emperor is wearing a laurel wreath on his head as a symbol of power.

Eques

The equites (singular: eques) were the middle class. Originally they were the horsemen of the army. They became very powerful and helped run the empire. This eques is wearing a helmet and body armor.

Plebian

Ordinary people were called plebians, or plebes. They worked in shops or as craftspeople. This plebian is wearing a brown cloak tunic and holding a hammer.

Dotty Nero

Join the dots to reveal the cruel Emperor Nero, then color him in. He loved music, poetry, and acting, but he killed a lot of people he didn't like, including his mother and his wife!

Emperor wordsearch

Can you find the following Roman emperors in the puzzle?

Augustus
Tiberius
Caligula
Claudius
Nero
Vespasian
Trajan
Hadrian
Diocletian

```
V A S Y W D I K U F L T P
V E S P A S I A N O I
G R G U S T M J X T R B T
E H Q H D E L R U N A J E C T
O G A U G U S T U S E N E R O R P
F L P D V T R D K Y Z L U B I G A X R
V R U R M I U J H A R O S C U O J P S
X N I O B W C L A U D I U S L A O
G A N O H D I O C L E T I A N
N X T A H E K N S H X L E
C A L I G U L A T J U
C U X E R F C
T J M A X
```

Odd coins out

Roman coins often had pictures of the emperor stamped on one side and buildings or symbols on the other. Which of these are the odd ones out?

Count like a Roman

Roman numbers (numerals) were based on seven letters:

I = 1   V = 5   X = 10   L = 50   C = 100   D = 500   M = 1000

You put the letters together to make numbers, but they had a few tricky rules about how to do this...

NO MORE than three of the same symbols in a row.

For example, III = 3

If the larger value letter is on the RIGHT, we subtract the letters before it.

For example, IV = 4

If the larger value letter is on the LEFT, we add the other letters to it.

For example, VI = 6

See if you can work out what these numbers are:

XIV =

VIII =

LXX =

XC =

Now do these math problems. You can write your answers in Roman numerals if you like!

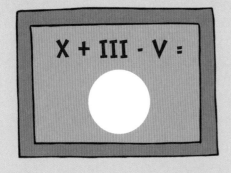

X + III - V =

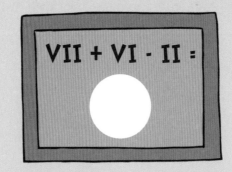

VII + VI - II =

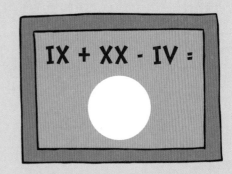

IX + XX - IV =

Roman timekeeping

The Romans used sundials to tell the time. An upright stick called a gnomon casts a shadow onto a pre-marked sundial face. As the sun moves across the sky, the shadow moves, too. Follow the instructions below to make your own sundial.

Ask a grown-up to help!

You'll need:

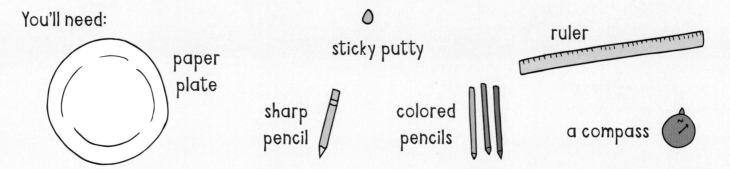

paper plate

sticky putty

ruler

sharp pencil

colored pencils

a compass

1. Mark the back of the plate into 12 equal sections. The easiest way to do this is to mark each quarter point first with a ruler and pencil, then add two points between each quarter.

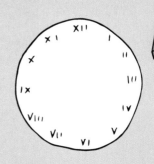

2. Use colored pencils or pens to write numbers around the circle to resemble a clock face. Use Roman numerals, starting with I for 1 and ending with XII for 12.

3. Find and mark the center of the plate using a ruler, then place a piece of sticky putty on the other side. Push the sharp end of the pencil through the plate into the putty to make the gnomon.

4. Place the sundial in a sunny spot on the ground so that a shadow is cast onto it.

5. Find north with the compass. Line up the XII at the top of the sundial with north. If the sun is shining, you should be able to tell the time! Here the time is 3 o'clock.

Dress like a Roman

Make a knee-length tunic and a bulla so you can dress up like a Roman child. A bulla was a small bag that children wore around their necks. It contained a lucky charm to protect them from evil spirits.

Ask a grown-up to help!

You'll need:

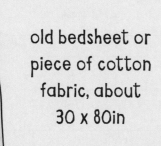
old bedsheet or piece of cotton fabric, about 30 x 80in

scissors

pins

needle and thread

rope or fabric belt

lucky charm, such as a very small toy animal

circular piece of felt, about 8in diameter

piece of string or narrow ribbon, about 30in long

TO MAKE THE TUNIC

1. Fold the fabric in half lengthwise, then cut out a semicircle on the folded edge to make room for your head.

2. Pin and sew down the long sides, leaving space for the armholes.

3. Turn the material inside out and put it on. Tie the tunic at your waist with a piece of rope or a fabric belt.

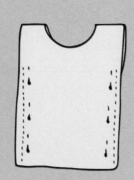

TO MAKE THE BULLA

1. Cut small holes around the edge of the felt. Thread the string or ribbon through the holes and draw tight to make a pouch.

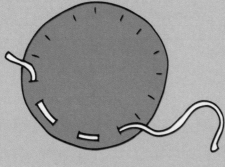

2. Put the lucky charm in the pouch. Knot the cord so you can wear it around your neck. To complete your outfit, put on a pair of sandals!

Party time

Dress up Empress Livia and her friends with stickers.

People carriers

Rich Romans were carried around town in a box called a litter. Can you spot five differences between these two pictures?

At the baths

Roman towns had large public baths with hot and cold pools and steam rooms. Men and women used the baths at different times to get clean and meet their friends. There was no soap, so they rubbed olive oil on their bodies and scraped it off. They could exercise in the gym, play games, and buy food and drink. Use stickers from the pages in the center of the book to complete this scene.

Disappearing Diana

Help! Diana, goddess of the hunt and moon, is fading away. Draw around her outlines, then color in the picture, too.

Fast fleet

Do the math to see which is the fastest warship. Write your answers on the sails.
The highest number is the fastest boat.

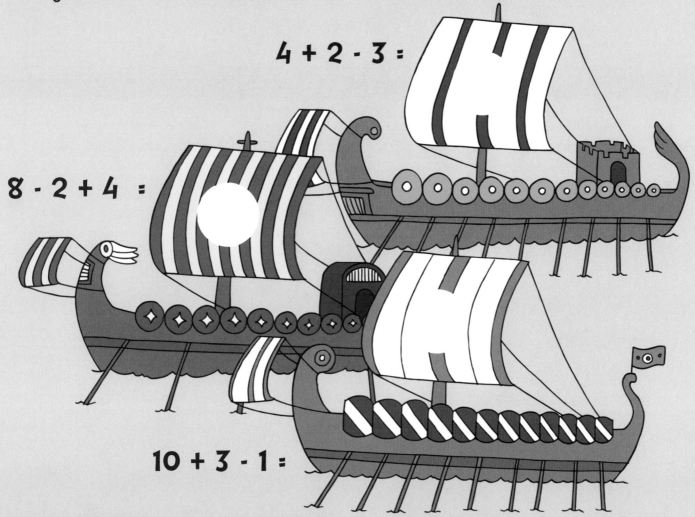

4 + 2 - 3 =

8 - 2 + 4 =

10 + 3 - 1 =

Odd shield out

Which one of these shields is the odd one out?
When you've worked that out, color them all in.

What's for dinner?

Rich Romans ate some strange food as well as things we would eat today.
They lay down to eat, and they ate mostly with their fingers. Check the list
to see what's missing from the picture. Add some stickers if you like, too.

Wild boar
Peacocks
Lobsters
Fish
Meat
Bread
Oysters
Apples
Cheese
Eggs
Snails

Make a laurel wreath

Laurel wreaths were a symbol of victory or honor and were often worn by emperors. Follow these instructions to look like a Caesar!

Ask a grown-up to help!

You'll need:

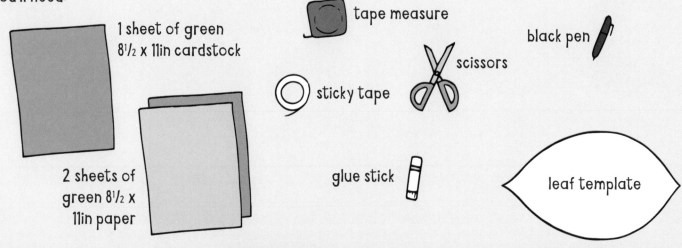

1 sheet of green 8½ x 11in cardstock

2 sheets of green 8½ x 11in paper

tape measure

sticky tape

scissors

glue stick

black pen

leaf template

1. Cut 3 x 1½in-wide strips across the width of the card and stick them together to make one long strip of card.

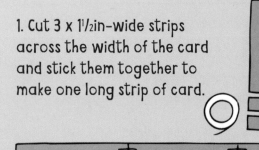

2. Put the card strip around your head and trim to fit, leaving an extra inch each side to overlap the two ends, but do not join together yet.

3. Trace over the leaf template and cut it out. Follow the outline of the leaf to draw and cut out about 40 leaf shapes from the paper.

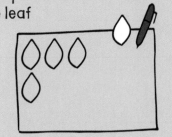

4. Glue one leaf about an inch from one end of the card strip, at an angle with the stem end at the bottom.

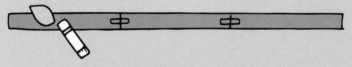

5. Glue a second leaf over the first, pointing downward.

6. Glue a third leaf over the second, pointing upward.

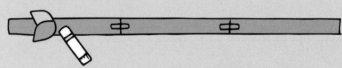

9. Put it on your head!

7. Continue gluing leaves pointing alternately up and down until you reach the final inch of the other end of the strip.

8. Tape the ends of the card strip together.

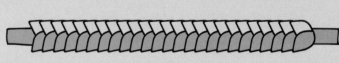

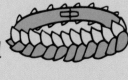

Great gods

Find the 12 major gods and goddesses hidden in the wordsearch.

JUPITER
JUNO
NEPTUNE
MINERVA
MARS
VENUS
APOLLO
DIANA
VULCAN
MERCURY
CERES
BACCHUS

```
A S T Y O L D R A J U P I T E R S
K N E R U V N M B I R S J D U A L
C D I A N A S J U O H O U Q E C V
I Q A S X Z G F W O A K T V U E F
N B L J H P O C B N P E T U A R H
O L K U M O M B U E K J D L J U A
R B J N M L L R E P W R F C D S R
Y A P O L L O S I T T V N A V M Y
N C U C Q T J M W U E O K N H N D
B C G M I N D E U N O L V X K Z K
V H A G N M M I N E R V A S Z D V
A U Z D C L Y J S D M D Q A W U E
S S X L O I T E B N H C V S P M N
T M A R S O H L J K L Z Q P J M U
A P L E R E C M E R C U R Y A G S
S O P U H L B W J G B H T O E B L
```

Doggie differences

In Roman mythology, Cerberus was a three-headed dog that guarded the entrance to the Underworld (the place where the Romans thought your spirit went after you died). Can you spot five differences between these two pictures?

Roman religion

The Romans worshipped many gods and goddesses, and each had their own temple. Priests wore white and killed animals on special days to please the gods. How many of the following can you see in the Temple of Juno? Add some stickers if you like.

Geese ◯

Priests ◯

Sheep ◯

Urns ◯

Rats ◯

Make a mosaic

The Romans decorated their homes with pictures and patterns called mosaics. These were made from small pieces of stone or pottery. Make your own mosaic by following the instructions below.

Ask a grown-up to help!

You'll need:

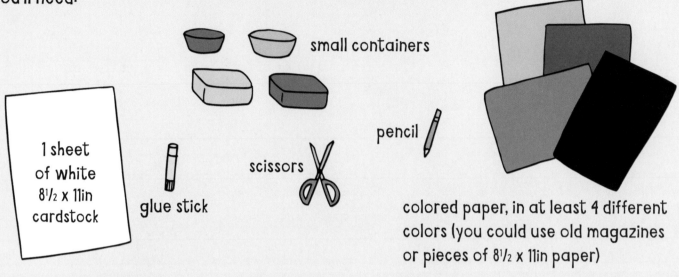

1 sheet of white 8½ x 11in cardstock

glue stick

scissors

pencil

small containers

colored paper, in at least 4 different colors (you could use old magazines or pieces of 8½ x 11in paper)

1. Cut the colored paper into strips about ½in wide and then into squares.

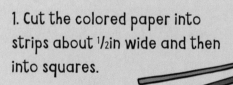

2. Organize the paper squares into different containers for each color.

3. Copy the design of a fish (see opposite) onto the white card, or draw your own design.

4. Cover a small section with glue.

5. Start filling in the design with the colored pieces of paper, leaving small gaps in between each one.

6. Continue filling in more sections with colored squares. Don't forget to fill in the background and the border around the design.

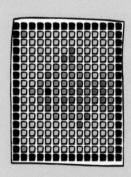

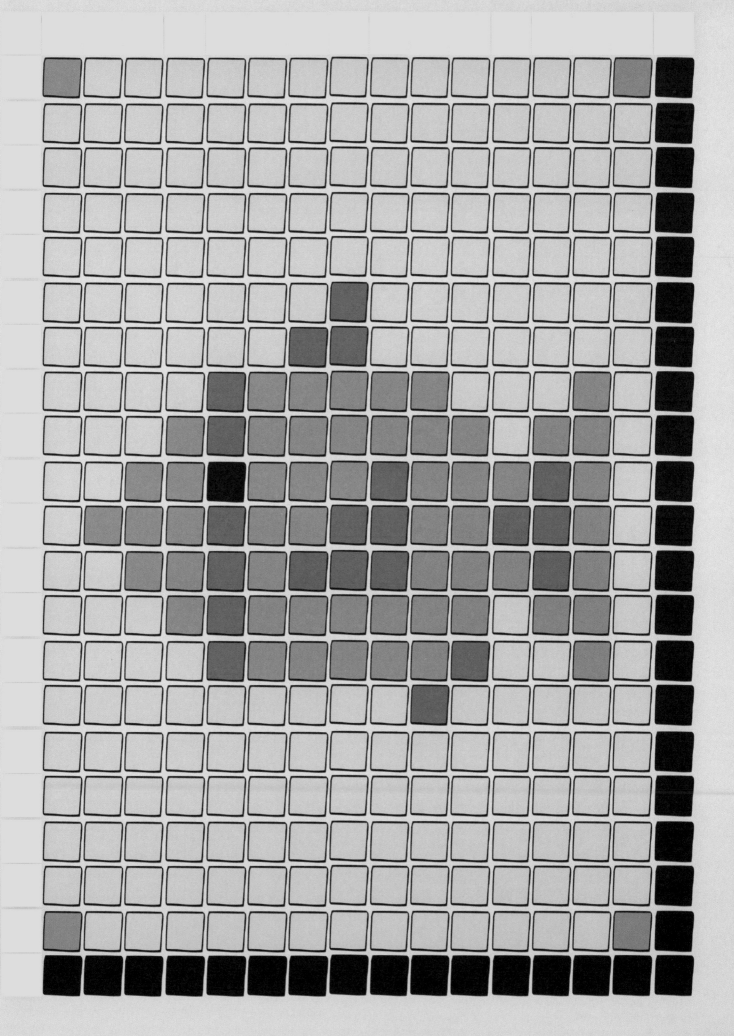

Election victory

Which of these citizens is going to win the election? Do the math to find out who has the most votes. If you were a slave or a woman, you couldn't vote or be voted for!

$4 + 6 - 2 =$ $9 + 2 - 1 =$ $5 - 3 + 4 =$

Off to the Senate

Help Julius Caesar get to the Senate so he can make a speech. Make sure he doesn't meet any trouble on the way!

Up for auction

Slaves were bought and sold throughout the Roman Empire. Which of these slaves is going to be bought at the slave market? He's wearing a green tunic and brown leggings, and he has short blond hair and a beard.

Slaving away

Unscramble the words to find out some of the different jobs that slaves did in Ancient Rome.

OKOC   _ _ _ _

TROIGLAAD   _ _ _ _ _ _ _ _ _

SHERERSDIAR   _ _ _ _ _ _ _ _ _ _

CHEERAT   _ _ _ _ _ _ _

OTCRA   _ _ _ _ _

ORCTOD   _ _ _ _ _ _

RIMEN   _ _ _ _ _

RENEDARG   _ _ _ _ _ _ _ _

MINER
GARDENER
GLADIATOR
DOCTOR
TEACHER
ACTOR
COOK
HAIRDRESSER

Fighting fit

Legionaries were the very best Roman soldiers. Can you use these descriptions to number the parts of this legionary's outfit?

❶ Sandals

He wore leather sandals and marched up to 30 miles a day.

❷ Belt and tunic

A leather belt held a dagger and sword and had dangling straps at the front for extra protection. It was worn over a knee-length red tunic.

❸ Helmet

This head protection had cheek pieces and a neckguard to protect from sword blows.

❹ Body armor

Made from overlapping iron strips, this enabled him to move around freely.

❺ Weapons

A legionary carried two javelins, a short sword, and a dagger.

❻ Scarf

This protected the neck from chafing caused by contact with the armor.

❼ Satchel

This leather bag was used to store rations in (usually salt and porridge).

❽ Shield

A painted shield made of wood, leather, and metal protected the body.

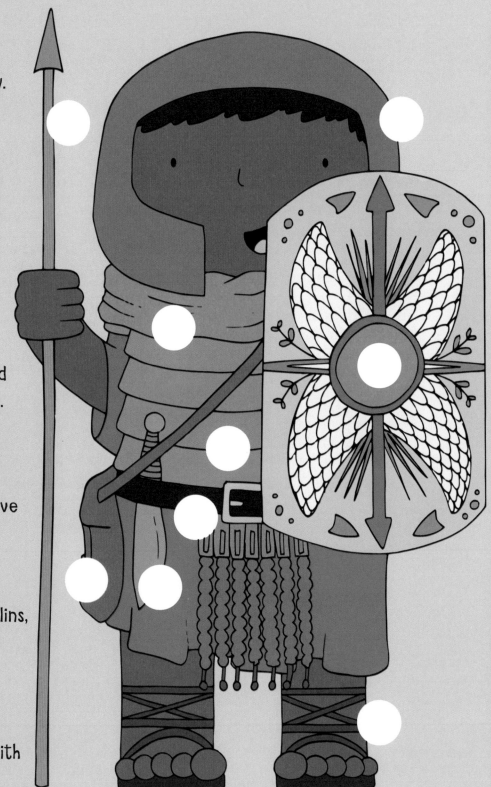

28

Disappearing standards

Soldiers were organized into large groups called legions and smaller groups called centuries. A standard was a long pole with badges or flags that represented the legion or century. These standards and soldiers are vanishing in the mist! Go over the outlines and then color them in to make them reappear.

On the road

The Romans were famous for building straight roads. Follow the Roman roads to help the Ninth Legion travel from Exeter back to their barracks at Hadrian's Wall.

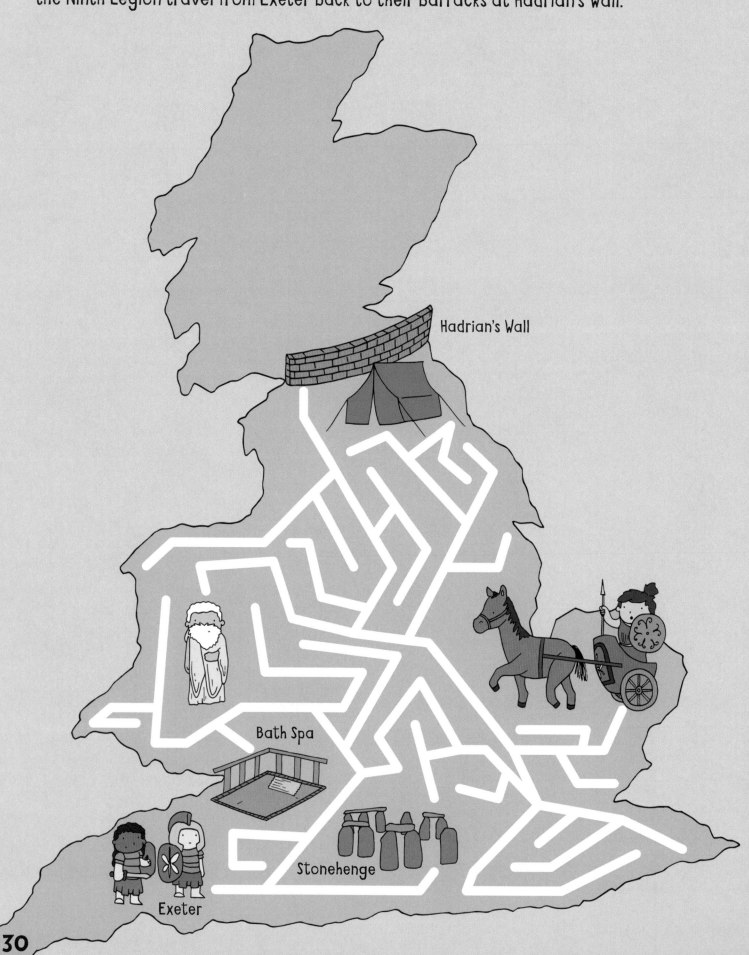

Hadrian's Wall

Bath Spa

Stonehenge

Exeter

Dotty centurion's helmet

A centurion was an officer in charge of a century. He had a crest on his helmet so that his men could follow him when fighting. Complete this dot to dot to reveal the centurion's helmet and then color it in.

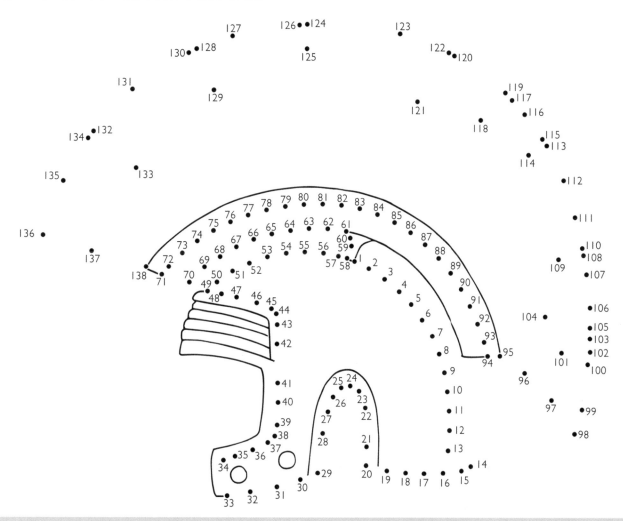

Silly soldiers

Who refereed the tennis match between Claudius and Vespasian?
A Roman umpire.

Why did the Romans build straight roads?
So their soldiers didn't go round the bend.

Where would you find Hadrian's Wall?
Around his garden.

Inside a Roman camp

A camp kept soldiers and their equipment safe. In summer, when they were fighting and marching, they built a new camp every night and lived in tents. How many soldiers can you spot? Color in this picture to complete the scene.

Battle scene counting

The Romans are off to fight the Celts. How many of the following can you see in the picture?

Javelins ⬤

Swords ⬤

Shields ⬤

Daggers ⬤

Battling Britons

The Romans had lots of enemies, including the English warrior queen Boudicea.
Can you find the five differences between these two pictures?

Express delivery

Do the math problems to find out who is the fastest messenger of the gods.

3 + 5 - 1 =

6 + 2 + 1 =

9 - 2 + 4 =

Fun and games

The Romans loved to watch people fight to the death in large, open-air venues called amphitheaters. The most famous amphitheater is the Colosseum in Rome. Use stickers from the center of the book to complete this picture.

Which weapon?

People who fought in the amphitheater were called gladiators. Can you match these gladiators to their weapons? Follow the tangled lines.

MURMILLO
This armored fighter wore a fish-shaped helmet.

RETIARIUS
This fighter wore very little armor and used a net.

GLADIATRIX
Women sometimes fought in the arena. It was a nasty job!

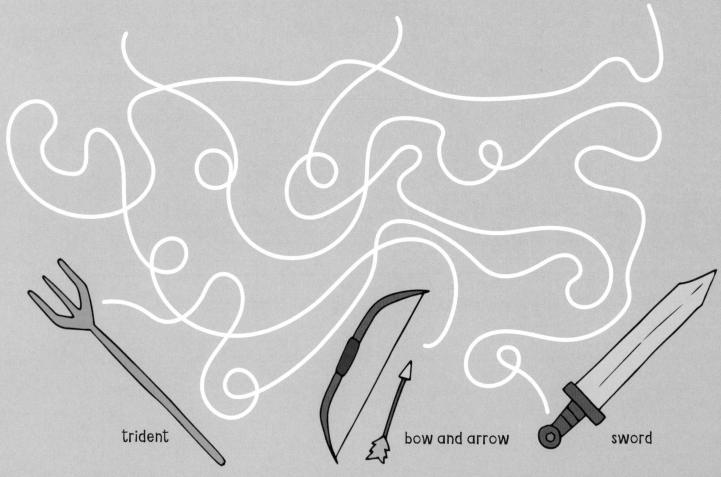

trident

bow and arrow

sword

Make gladiator weapons

Here's how to make a round gladiator shield and sword. Make a set for yourself and a friend, and stage your own gladiatorial combat!

You'll need:

Thick cardboard (or an old cardboard box)

scissors

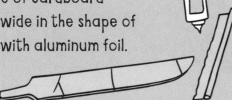
aluminum foil

paints and paintbrush

glue

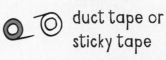
colored duct tape or sticky tape

ruler

Ask a grown-up to help!

sheet of cardstock

TO MAKE THE SWORD

1. Cut out a piece of cardboard about 16 x 1½in wide in the shape of a sword. Cover with aluminum foil.

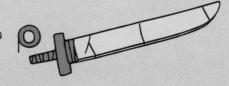

2. Cut out a piece of cardstock about 6 x 4in to make a handguard. Cut a slit in the middle of the card, a little wider than the sword blade.

3. Slide the handguard down onto the sword until it is a couple of inches from the bottom of the sword. Wrap colored duct tape above and below the handguard to keep it in place.

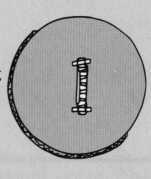

TO MAKE THE SHIELD

1. Cut out a circle of cardboard about 14in in diameter. Cut a rectangular slot about 5½ x 1in in the middle of it.

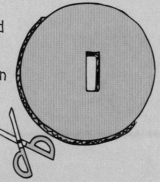

2. Cut a strip of cardstock about 8 x 1in. Cover in duct tape then push it through the slot to make a handle, taping down the ends on the other side.

3. Cut out a circle of cardstock about 6in in diameter. Cut out a triangle shape and roll the remainder of the card circle into a cone. Glue it together, then stick the cone to the center of the shield to make a boss (this helps to deflect sword blows).

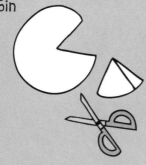

4. Paint the front of the shield and get ready for action!

39

Animals in the arena

Wild beast hunts were held in the arena, and sometimes the emperor joined in!
Find the pairs of animals and color them in to match.

Keeping it fresh

An amphora was a large pottery storage jar with handles.
Which one of these holds the most wine? Do the math to find out.

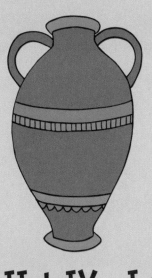

II + IV - I :

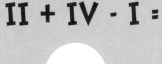

V + III + I :

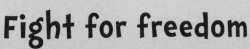

IX - I + VI :

Fight for freedom

A gladiator who won several fights was allowed to retire.
Which one of these will receive the wooden sword and their
freedom from the emperor? He has brown hair, is wearing
a helmet, and is carrying a round shield.

Cursed luck

In Roman times there was no police force, so the victims of crimes wrote "curse tablets" (defixios) asking the gods for their help instead. Curse tablets were messages scratched on scraps of lead. Choose from the words in the list to complete this one.

To the god _____

Two of my _____ have been stolen. I ask that the _____ lose the power of _____ and make a _____ like a sheep for the rest of his life.

Thank you very much!

Marcus Publius Antoninus

SPEECH

NOISE

NEPTUNE

THIEF

SHEEP

Make a Roman bracelet

Jewelry was very important to women because it was their own property and they could do what they wanted with it. Solid-gold snake bracelets were popular items, worn around the wrist or the upper arm. Follow the instructions below to make one.

Ask a grown-up to help!

You'll need:

small cardboard tube, such as an empty toilet paper roll

scissors

marker

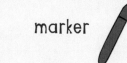

pencil or pen

gold paint and paintbrush

1. Draw a snake onto the cardboard tube so that it coils around the length.

2. Paint it gold. Leave to dry, then cut it out.

3. Add features using the marker.

4. Wear it!

Roman jokes

How did the Romans cut their hair?
With a pair of Caesars.

Which famous Roman suffered from hayfever?
Julius Sneezer.

Where did Caesar keep his armies?
Up his sleevies.

43

Catapult math

When the Roman army invaded a country, it attacked with special weapons. Roman catapults used heavy rocks to smash through walls and fortifications. Which one of these can fire the rocks the farthest? Do the math problems to find out.

12 - 5 + 3 =

3 + 6 + 2 =

8 - 4 + 8 =

Divine differences

Minerva was the Roman goddess of wisdom and warfare.
Can you spot five differences between these two pictures of her?

Find the lost Roman standards

Each legion carried a silver or bronze eagle standard (aquila) as a symbol of its power. If the aquila was captured by the enemy, it was a terrible disgrace, and the legion broke up. Can you find the five lost aquilas in the forest?

Marching in the streets

The triumph was a great parade held to celebrate a major military victory. It ended with a sacrifice to the god Jupiter and a big party. Choose stickers from the pages in the middle of this book to complete the scene.

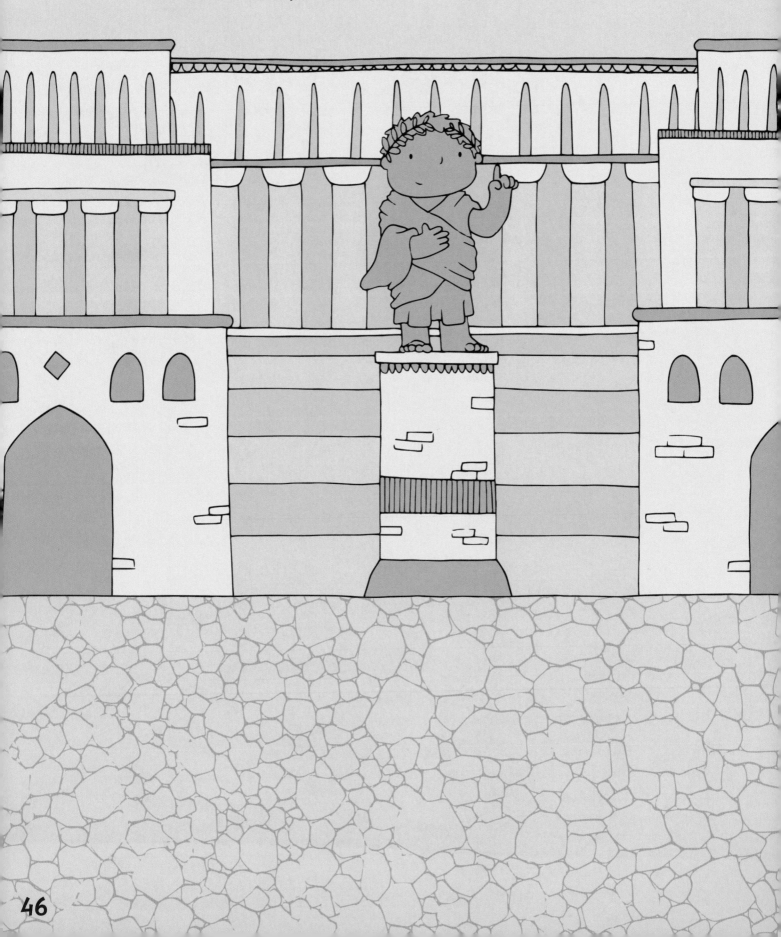

Kill or cure

The Romans had lots of remedies for illnesses, but some were a bit silly or horrid! Match the number to the Roman numeral (see page 10) to find the cure for each illness.

ILLNESS

V   Cut or wound

VIII   Epilepsy

X   Toothache

IX   Sneezing

VII   Nausea

III   Fever

I   Pimples

VI   Headache

IV   Common cold

II   Upset tummy

CURE

1   Slab of crocodile meat

2   Raw egg yolks

3   Cucumber

4   Hot pepper

5   Wool, dipped in wine

6   Laurel wreath

7   Drink lots of wine

8   Dried camel's brain

9   Kiss the nose of a mule

10   Mouthwash of vinegar and boiled frogs

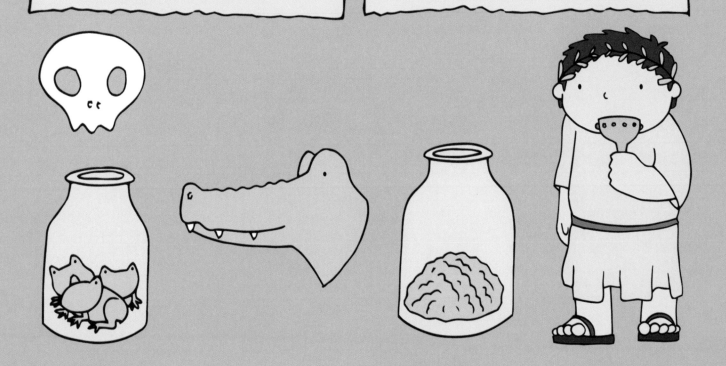

735 BC

river

Mars

fight

brothers

wolf

city

babies

Neptune

Vesta

Mars

Jupiter

Venus

Juno

worried

angry

sad

happy

Secret messages

When Julius Caesar was trying to take over the world, he wrote to his generals in code. This meant his enemies didn't know what he was planning! Using the alphabet code, can you work out this message? Write the letters underneath. Some of the letters have been done for you.

A=D B=E C=F D=G E=H F=I G=J H=K I=L J=M
K=N L=O M=P N=Q O=R P=S Q=T R=U S=V
T=W U=X V=Y W=Z X=A Y=B Z=C

To: Quintus Rufius Maximus, Commander, XI Legion,
Somewhere in France

Greetings, Quintus

D w w d f n   w r p r u u r z   d w   g d z q!
A t _ _ c _   _ o _ _ r _ _ w   _ t   _ _ _ n!

Good luck,
Julius Caesar

Then can you complete the message sent back to him, putting some of the words in code? Scribble out the words in gray when you've finished.

Hail, Caesar!

Great news! Only _ _ _ _ _ _ of our men are _ _ _ _.
                twenty   dead

Uptohistrix has fled to _ _ _ _ _. I am following.
                              Paris

Best wishes, Quintus

Reflective Romans

There were many famous Roman poets, thinkers, and historians. See if you can find the following in the wordsearch.

VIRGIL

SENECA

OVID

HORACE

PTOLEMY

JUVENAL

CICERO

PLINY

CATULLUS

TACITUS

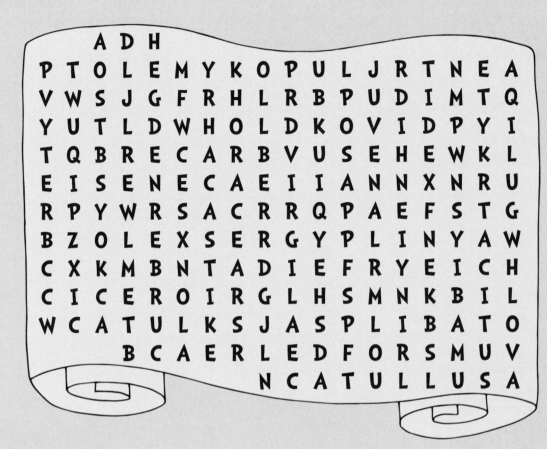

```
      A D H
P T O L E M Y K O P U L J R T N E A
V W S J G F R H L R B P U D I M T Q
Y U T L D W H O L D K O V I D P Y I
T Q B R E C A R B V U S E H E W K L
E I S E N E C A E I I A N N X N R U
R P Y W R S A C R R Q P A E F S T G
B Z O L E X S E R G Y P L I N Y A W
C X K M B N T A D I E F R Y E I C H
C I C E R O I R G L H S M N K B I L
W C A T U L K S J A S P L I B A T O
    B C A E R L E D F O R S M U V
      N C A T U L L U S A
```

The color of power

The Romans boiled up sea snails to make a purple dye. It was very expensive, and only rich people could afford it. Can you guess how many snails were needed to dye the edge of one toga? Circle the number you think is right. Then draw lines to match the pairs of snails and color them in.

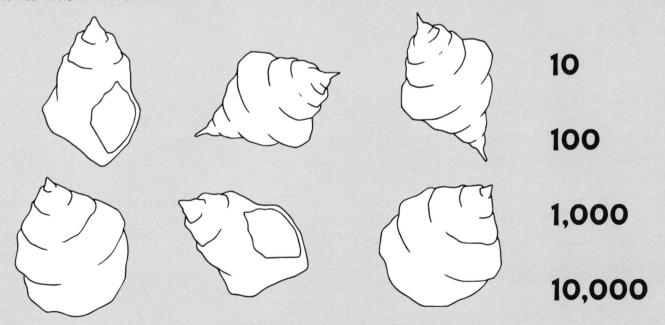

10

100

1,000

10,000

Putting on an act

The Romans loved going to the theater. Plays were held in open-air venues. Actors were men who wore masks with big, bold expressions. This told the audience how each character was feeling. Go over the outlines of these masks and then color them in. Put a sticker with the word angry, happy, worried, or sad by each one.

Name that god

See if you can match these gods to the descriptions below. Put a sticker of the correct name by each one, or write in the boxes.

JUPITER
God of the sky and chief god, holding a thunderbolt.

VESTA
Goddess of the home, carrying a torch.

VENUS
Goddess of love, carrying flowers.

MARS
God of war, dressed for battle.

JUNO
Jupiter's wife and protector of Rome.

NEPTUNE
God of the sea, carrying a trident.

A day at the races

Chariot racing was very dangerous and hugely popular. The Circus Maximus (the racing stadium) in Rome had room for 250,000 people! There were four teams: the reds, whites, blues, and greens. Color in the horses' saddle cloths to match the chariots, but leave the white team blank. Then do the math to see which team will win.

7 + 6 - 5 =

3 + 2 + 1 =

8 - 4 + 6 =

1 + 7 - 2 =

Ship shape

Roman warships (galley ships) needed lots of people to row them. Can you match the ship to the silhouette?

Making music

Which is Emperor Nero's favorite musical instrument?
Follow the tangled lines to find out.

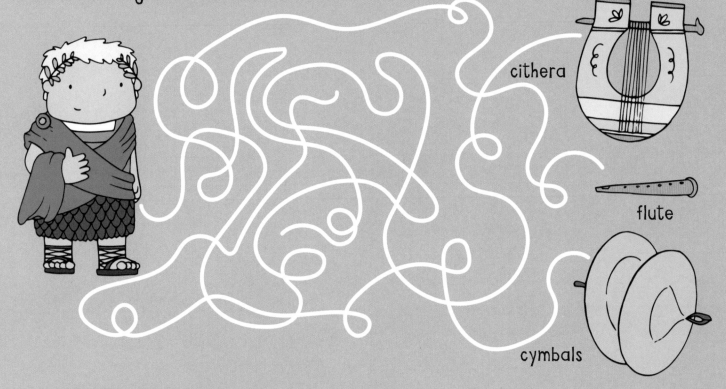

cithera

flute

cymbals

Make some libum

Libum was a special bread made as an offering to the household gods. This is a modern version of a Roman recipe.

Ask a grown-up to help!

You'll need:

5oz ricotta cheese

mixing bowl

6 bay leaves

1 egg, beaten

baking sheet

½ cup flour, sifted, plus extra if needed

wooden spoon

parchment paper

2 tbsp honey

1. Preheat the oven to 350°F. Put the ricotta cheese into a mixing bowl and beat with a wooden spoon until soft.

2. Add the beaten egg and mix well.

3. Slowly add the flour and stir gently to make a dough (add more flour if the mixture is too sticky).

4. Divide the dough into two balls and then flatten into ½in-thick loaves.

5. Place on a baking sheet lined with parchment paper with 3 bay leaves underneath each loaf.

6. Bake for 30-40 minutes or until golden brown and cooked through.

7. Spread the tops of the loaves with honey and let stand until warm to the touch.

8. Remove the bay leaves from the underside of each loaf before serving.

City life

We know a lot about the Romans because a volcano, Mount Vesuvius, erupted in 79 AD. covering the city of Pompeii with hot ash and lava. This destroyed the city but also preserved it. Today archaeologists are still digging up things from Pompeii that tell us about how people lived in Roman times. Towns and cities were very crowded, and most people lived in apartment blocks above stores. Color in this busy street scene in Pompeii.

Find the Roman villa (page 4)

What the Romans did for us (page 5)

Aqueduct

Alphabet

Daily news

Months of the year

Public toilets

Who's who in Ancient Rome (pages 6-7)

Emperor   Patricians

Eques   Plebian   Slave

Emperor wordsearch (page 9)

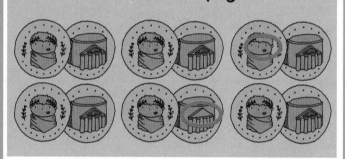

```
V A S Y W D I K U F L T P
V E S P A S I A N O I
G R G U S T M J X T R B T
E H Q H D E L R U N A J E C T
O G A U G U S T U S E N E R O R P
F L P D V T R D K Y Z L U B I G A X R
V R U R M I U J H A R O S C U O J P S
X N I O B W C L A U D I U S L A O
G A N O H D I O C L E T I A N
N X T A H E K N S H X L E
C A L I G U L A T J U
C U X E R F C
T J M A X
```

Odd coins out (page 9)

Count like a Roman (page 10)

XIV = 14

VIII = 8

LXX = 70

XC = 90

| 8 | 11 | 25 |

People carriers (page 13)

Fast fleet (page 17)

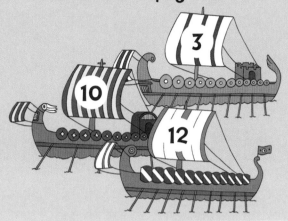

Odd shield out (page 17)

What's for dinner? (pages 18-19)

Missing: peacocks and eggs.

Great gods (page 21)

Doggie differences (page 21)

Roman religion (pages 22-23)

Geese = 5   Urns = 5
Priests = 3   Rats = 8
Sheep = 4

Election victory (page 26)

Off to the Senate (page 26)

Up for auction (page 27)

Slaving away (page 27)

Cook
Gladiator
Hairdresser
Teacher
Actor
Doctor
Miner
Gardener

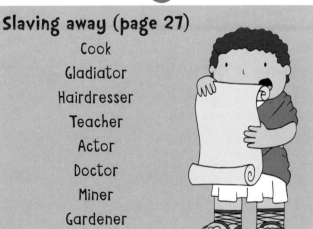

Fighting fit (page 28)

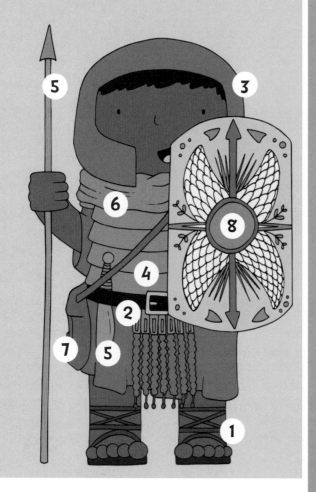

On the road (page 30)

Inside a Roman camp (pages 32-33)

There are 9 soldiers.

Battle scene counting (page 34)

Javelins = 2
Swords = 5
Shields = 17
Daggers = 2

Battling Britons (page 35)

Express delivery (page 35)

7   9   11

Which weapon? (page 38)

Animals in the arena (page 40)

Keeping it fresh (page 41)

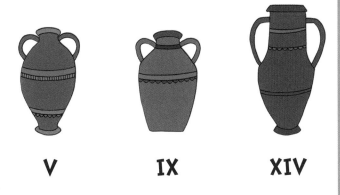

V   IX   XIV

Fight for freedom (page 41)

Cursed luck (page 42)

To the god NEPTUNE

Two of my SHEEP have been stolen. I ask that the THIEF lose the power of SPEECH and make a NOISE like a sheep for the rest of his life.

Thank you very much!

Marcus Publius Antoninus

Catapult math (page 44)

10   11   12

Divine differences (page 44)

Find the lost Roman standard (page 45)

Kill or cure (page 48)

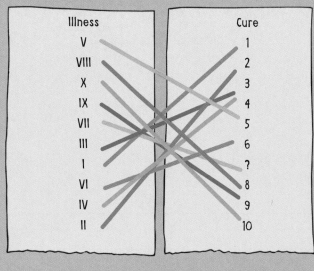

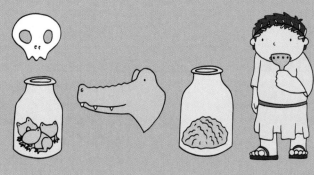

Reflective Romans (page 50)

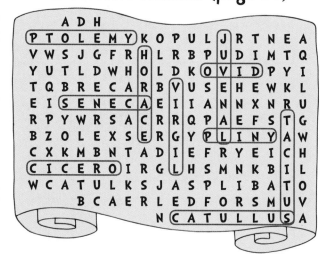

The color of power (page 50)

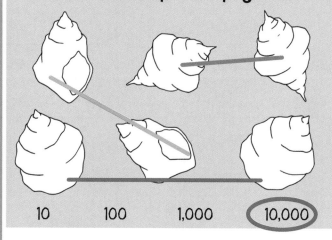

10   100   1,000   (10,000)

Secret messages (page 49)

To: Quintus Rufius Maximus, Commander, XI Legion, Somewhere in France

Greetings, Quintus

ATTACK   TOMORROW   AT   DAWN!

Good luck,
Julius Caesar

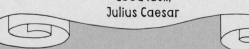

Hail, Caesar!

Great news! Only W Z H Q W B of our men are G H D G. Uptohistrix has fled to S D U L V. I am following.

Best wishes, Quintus

Putting on an act (page 51)

Angry

Worried

Happy   Sad

Name that god (page 52)

Jupiter

Juno

Venus

Neptune

Mars

Vesta

A day at the races (page 53)

8

6

10

6

Ship shape (page 54)

Making music (page 54)

First published 2020 by Button Books, an imprint of Guild of Master Craftsman Publications Ltd, Castle Place, 166 High Street, Lewes, East Sussex, BN7 1XU, UK. Text © GMC Publications Ltd, 2020. Copyright in the Work © GMC Publications Ltd, 2020. Illustrations © 2020 Jennifer Alliston. ISBN 978 1 78708 043 0. Distributed by Publishers Group West in the United States. All rights reserved. The right of Jennifer Alliston to be identified as the illustrator of this work has been asserted in accordance with the Copyright, Designs, and Patents Act 1988, sections 77 and 78. No part of this publication may be reproduced, stored in a retrieval system, or transmitted in any form or by any means without the prior permission of the publisher and copyright owner. While every effort has been made to obtain permission from the copyright holders for all material used in this book, the publishers will be pleased to hear from anyone who has not been appropriately acknowledged and to make the correction in future reprints. The publishers and author can accept no legal responsibility for any consequences arising from the application of information, advice, or instructions given in this publication. A catalog record for this book is available from the British Library. Publisher: Jonathan Bailey. Production: Jim Bulley and Jo Pallett. Senior Project Editor: Sara Harper. Managing Art Editor: Gilda Pacitti. Color origination by GMC Reprographics. Printed and bound in China. Warning! Choking hazard—small parts. Not suitable for children under 3 years.